YOUTUBE PLANNING BOOK FOR KIDS

A NOTEBOOK FOR BUDDING YOUTUBERS

Vol. 3

Other titles in the series:

We publish extra volumes in different cover designs to suit taste and BUMPER Editions which have 30 planning pages, for really avid planners.

YouTube Planning Book for Kids Vol 1 (blue)

YouTube Planning Book for Kids Vol 2 (multicolour)

YouTube Planning Book for Kids BUMPER Edition

Minecraft Planning Book for Kids

Minecraft Planning Book for Kids BUMPER Edition

Vlogging Planning Book for Kids

Revised and Expanded 2nd Edition

ISBN: 978-1-912293-03-2

MY INFO

MY NAME:

NICKNAMES:

AGE:

THINGS I LIKE:

MY BEST MATES:

MY YOUTUBE NAME:

MY FAVOURITE YOUTUBERS:

WHY USE THIS BOOK?

▶ MAKE YOUR YOUTUBE VIDEOS BETTER!

▶ Keep a record of your videos so you know which ones are the most popular.

▶ **Keep a record of the topics you cover so you can make sure you don't do the same thing each time.**

▶ Show your parents how being a YouTuber can be good for your education...
it teaches you planning and organising, writing and storytelling, innovation, technology skills, editing skills, how to think about your target audience, and how to be safe whilst using the internet. How could they refuse?

▶ IF YOU MAKE LOADS OF EPIC VIDEOS AND GET LOTS OF VIEWERS YOU CAN START TO MAKE MONEY!

BEFORE YOU START:

CHOOSE WHAT TYPE of YouTuber you want to be? Do you want to focus on gaming? Do you want to be a vlogger where you are the star of the show? Do you want to focus on doing product reviews where you show new toys or gadgets and review them? Do you want to show stunts and tricks or skills (such as cool hairstyles or sports skills)

What EQUIPMENT will you use? Will you use a video-camera, a tablet or a camera phone, a web-cam or an action camera like a GoPro? Will you use a tripod or a selfie-stick to keep the camera steady? What editing software have you got?

Have you set up a YOUTUBE ACCOUNT? Choose your YouTube name. Not your real name, but something memorable. Decide on whether your YouTube channel will be private or public. If you are under 13 years old you will need your parents to set it up.

Don't forget SAFETY. Remember that everything shared on the Internet can me viewed by anybody - good or bad, kind or mean.

Keep your personal information (real name, age, address, school) PRIVATE. Agree with your parents if you are allowed to appear in your videos, or just a screen, or your hands, for example. Don't reply to comments that are unkind. Report these to YouTube immediately and ignore them. Speak to your parents about how you will use YouTube safely.

SHHH! FILMING IN PROGRESS
AND OTHER HINTS AND TIPS ON HOW TO MAKE COOL VIDEOS

Make a "Shhh! Filming in Progress" sign so you don't get interrupted by your parents or a brother or sister. *USE THIS ONE >>*

Make sure you have good lighting.

Make sure there isn't anything in the background you don't want people to see (like your messy bedroom or anything with personal information on it)

Don't have long pauses in the commentary. Plan what you're going to say in advance or do a voice-over afterwards, or use music.

Always have an opening phrase but think of ways to keep it fresh.

Always use your YouTube name.

Tell people what you're going to do in your video at the start and have a consistent ending.

Remind viewers to like and comment and subscribe.

Use editing software, like iMovie, to add music, time-lapse, slo-mo and voice-over.

Plan your video so it's successful first time

SHHH! FILMING IN PROGRESS

YOUTUBING HERO AT WORK ON

MASTERPIECES OF YOUTUBE GOLD

<<< DISTURB AT YOUR PERIL >>>

IDEA STORM

WHAT'S AN IDEA STORM? Think of all your favourite vlogs / youtube videos, or new ideas you've thought of. Use this space to write down all your ideas. You can come back to this space for inspiration when planning each of your new videos....

ALL THE STUFF I WANT TO YOUTUBE ABOUT

👍 PLANNING 101

*Things to think about to make each
video more focused and more brilliant*

What TYPE of VIDEO do YOU want TO make?

Some YouTubers will try out different types of video style before choosing what they enjoy most, what they're best at, and what gets the most likes, comments, subscribers. Here are some types to try:

PERSONAL VLOG - everyday videos about your own life, the key theme is you and your life! If your life is different to most people's this might be what makes it interesting. If it's not, this might not be for you.

PRODUCT REVIEWS - from unboxing (when you open a toy / gadget / book / game for the first time) to live demos about what it's like and how it works. People love to watch these when deciding whether to buy something. Make your review entertaining and full of information to get more likes! Choose popular products to get more hits (views).

GAMING - kids LOVE watching live computer games, the graphics and action are almost like watching a movie... but also to pick up hints and tips for the game that they can use themselves. Plan each video around a particular challenge / battle / skill / adventure that you think will be fun to share. Keep it focused and make sure the title includes the name of the game so it comes up in searches.

FUN AND PRANKS - if you have some funny or wacky ideas, making entertaining videos to make your viewers gasp or laugh can be a fun way to make YouTube success! Always make sure they are safe and not rude - you don't want to get a ban or be embarassed later on in your life.

STUNTS AND SKILLS - show off some of your best skills, bike stunts, gymnastics, parkour, fashion choices... use editing and music to make them really cool.

What WILL the TOPIC be?

Simple. Make sure you decide what each video is going to be about BEFORE you start filming! You'd be surprised how many don't and leads to messy, boring watching and NO LIKES!

The BEGINNING, The MIDDLE, and THE End!

Once you have an AWESOME TOPIC, plan how you are going to make your video EPIC too. Write a LIST, or draw pictures in a STORYBOARD showing the key things that will happen.

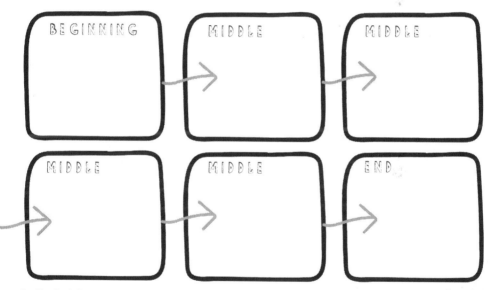

BEGINNING: Always plan how you will start your video. Make it upbeat and catchy so viewers keep on watching. Tell the viewers what's going to happen, so they decide to keep watching too!

MIDDLE: The bit where you show something, do something, say something about your chosen topic. Use editing to keep it interesting. You can chop and change camera angles, speed things up, slow them down, add music, add graphics. Choose wisely and see what works.

END: Be consistent, say it's The End and ask people to LIKE or COMMENT! Tell them what your next video will be about too.

The TITLE

When you've cracked your video and it's ready, think carefully about the words you use in the title. This is what viewers will read before they decide to watch your video. It's also what YouTube will use in the search box results. Make it as relevant as possible.

KEY WORDS If your video is about Minecraft, but you don't put that it's about Minecraft in the title, when people search for Minecraft they won't find your video. Get it?! Make sure the title has the words in it that people are searching for. If they can't find your video, they can't watch it.

BE DIFFERENT. There are millions of videos on YouTube and there will probably already be some about the same topic you've chosen. Make your title sound interesting to get them to watch your video rather than someone else's and hey presto - more views and more subscribers!

WHO is GOING to WATCH your VIDEOS?

Keep an eye on who your viewers are and read their comments. You might want to keep doing or change things about your videos once you know who is watching them!

HOW OLD Think about how old your viewers are and what interests them. Younger kids often like to watch videos by kids older than them. If you have younger kids watching your videos, make sure the content is right and that the words you use are simple and appropriate.

GIRLS OR BOYS You might get more girls watching your videos or vice versa. See if you can find out and choose topics you think they'll like to see more about.

WHERE THEY LIVE Working out where your viewers live might also give you new ideas for topics to cover. If viewers from other countries watch your videos you might want to make more videos about your own country as this might be what is interesting to them. Ask them!

NOW LET'S GET STARTED >

VIDEO NO. 1

TYPE OF VIDEO:

Vlog / Product Review / Gaming / Funny / Stunts and Skills

What will the topic be?

_____

_____

WHAT'S GOING TO HAPPEN?

How will it start?

What will happen in the middle?

How will it end?

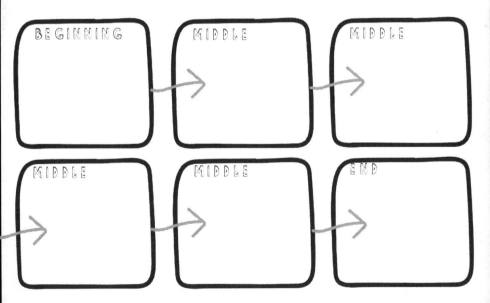

| BEGINNING | MIDDLE | MIDDLE |
| MIDDLE | MIDDLE | END |

What will the title be?

_____

WHO WILL VIEW IT?

What will they like about it? Why will they watch it?

_____

_____

_____

SUCCESS?

VIDEO STATS

Date uploaded: _____

Views ___ 👍 ___ 👎 ___

Shares ___   Comments ___   Subscribers ___

How would YOU rate your video out of 10? ____

Would you do anything differently next time?

_____

_____

VIDEO NO. 2

TYPE OF VIDEO:

Vlog / Product Review / Gaming / Funny / Stunts and Skills

What will the topic be?

_____

_____

WHAT'S GOING TO HAPPEN?

How will it start?

What will happen in the middle?

How will it end?

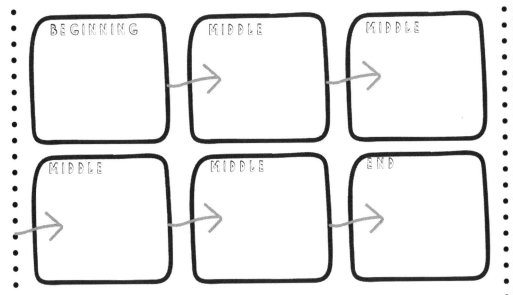

BEGINNING

MIDDLE

MIDDLE

MIDDLE

MIDDLE

END

What will the title be?

_____

WHO WILL VIEW IT?

What will they like about it? Why will they watch it?

_____

_____

_____

SUCCESS?

VIDEO STATS

Date uploaded: _____

Views ___   👍 ___   👎 ___

Shares ___   Comments ___   Subscribers ___

How would YOU rate your video out of 10? ____

Would you do anything differently next time?

_____

_____

VIDEO NO. 3

TYPE OF VIDEO:

Vlog / Product Review / Gaming / Funny / Stunts and Skills

What will the topic be?

_____

_____

WHAT'S GOING TO HAPPEN?

How will it start?

What will happen in the middle?

How will it end?

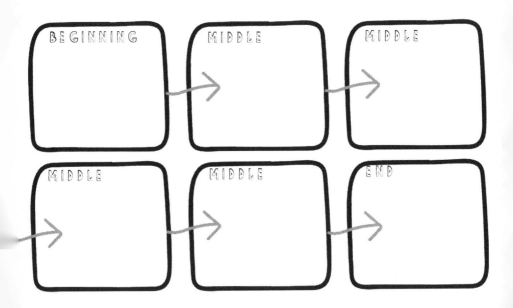

BEGINNING	MIDDLE	MIDDLE

MIDDLE	MIDDLE	END

What will the title be?

_____

WHO WILL VIEW IT?

What will they like about it? Why will they watch it?

_____

_____

_____

SUCCESS?

VIDEO STATS

Date uploaded: _____

Views ____ 👍 ____ 👎 ____

Shares ____   Comments ____   Subscribers ____

How would YOU rate your video out of 10? ____

Would you do anything differently next time?

_____

_____

VIDEO NO. 4

TYPE OF VIDEO:

Vlog / Product Review / Gaming / Funny / Stunts and Skills

What will the topic be?

_____

_____

WHAT'S GOING TO HAPPEN?

How will it start?

What will happen in the middle?

How will it end?

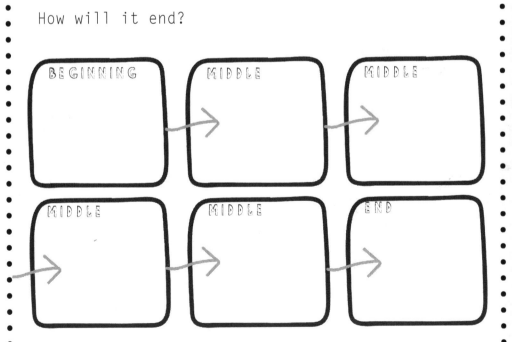

| BEGINNING | MIDDLE | MIDDLE |
| MIDDLE | MIDDLE | END |

What will the title be?

_____

WHO WILL VIEW IT?

What will they like about it? Why will they watch it?

_____

_____

_____

SUCCESS?

VIDEO STATS

Date uploaded: _____

Views ____   👍 ____   👎 ____

Shares ____   Comments ____   Subscribers ____

How would YOU rate your video out of 10? ____

Would you do anything differently next time?

_____

_____

VIDEO NO. 5

Vlog / Product Review / Gaming / Funny / Stunts and Skills

What will the topic be?

_____

_____

WHAT'S GOING TO HAPPEN?

How will it start?

What will happen in the middle?

How will it end?

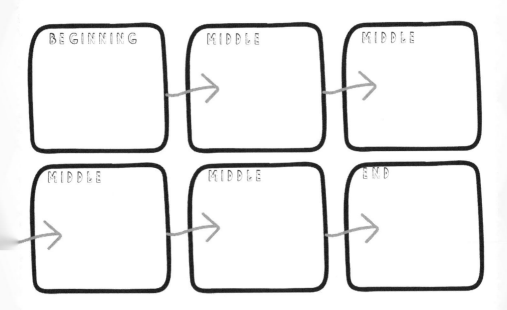

What will the title be?

WHO WILL VIEW IT?

What will they like about it? Why will they watch it?

SUCCESS?

VIDEO STATS

Date uploaded: _____

Views _____ 👍 _____ 👎 _____

Shares _____   Comments _____   Subscribers _____

How would YOU rate your video out of 10? _____

Would you do anything differently next time?

VIDEO NO. 6

TYPE OF VIDEO:

Vlog / Product Review / Gaming / Funny / Stunts and Skills

What will the topic be?

_____

_____

WHAT'S GOING TO HAPPEN?

How will it start?

What will happen in the middle?

How will it end?

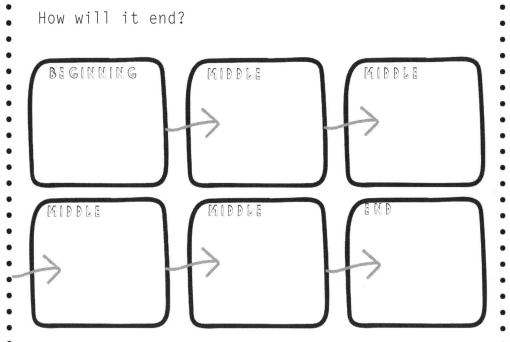

BEGINNING → MIDDLE → MIDDLE

MIDDLE → MIDDLE → END

What will the title be?

_____

WHO WILL VIEW IT?

What will they like about it? Why will they watch it?

_____

_____

_____

SUCCESS?

VIDEO STATS

Date uploaded: _____

Views ____   👍 ____   👎 ____

Shares ____   Comments ____   Subscribers ____

How would YOU rate your video out of 10? ____

Would you do anything differently next time?

_____

_____

VIDEO NO. 7

TYPE OF VIDEO:

Vlog / Product Review / Gaming / Funny / Stunts and Skills

What will the topic be?

_____

_____

WHAT'S GOING TO HAPPEN?

How will it start?

What will happen in the middle?

How will it end?

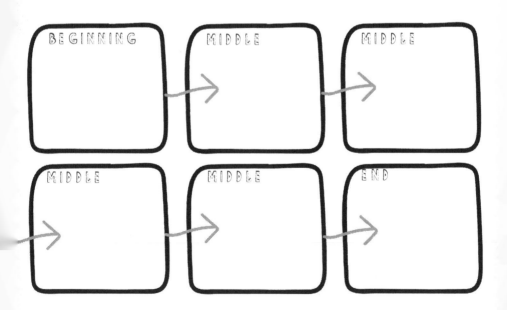

What will the title be?

_____

WHO WILL VIEW IT?

What will they like about it? Why will they watch it?

_____

_____

_____

SUCCESS?

VIDEO STATS

Date uploaded: _____

Views ____ 👍 ____ 👎 ____

Shares ____   Comments ____   Subscribers ____

How would YOU rate your video out of 10? ____

Would you do anything differently next time?

_____

_____

VIDEO NO. 8

TYPE OF VIDEO:

Vlog / Product Review / Gaming / Funny / Stunts and Skills

What will the topic be?

_____

_____

WHAT'S GOING TO HAPPEN?

How will it start?

What will happen in the middle?

How will it end?

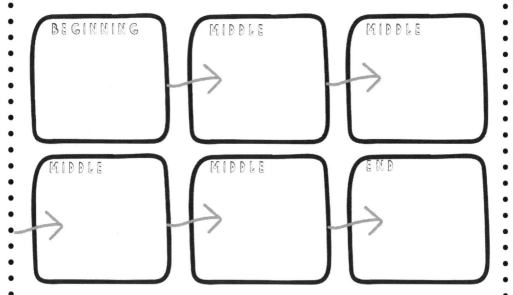

| BEGINNING | MIDDLE | MIDDLE |
| MIDDLE | MIDDLE | END |

What will the title be?

_____

WHO WILL VIEW IT?

What will they like about it? Why will they watch it?

_____

_____

_____

SUCCESS?

VIDEO STATS

Date uploaded: _____

Views ___ 👍 ___ 👎 ___

Shares ___   Comments ___   Subscribers ____

How would YOU rate your video out of 10? ____

Would you do anything differently next time?

_____

_____

VIDEO NO. 9

TYPE OF VIDEO:

Vlog / Product Review / Gaming / Funny / Stunts and Skills

What will the topic be?

_____

_____

WHAT'S GOING TO HAPPEN?

How will it start?

What will happen in the middle?

How will it end?

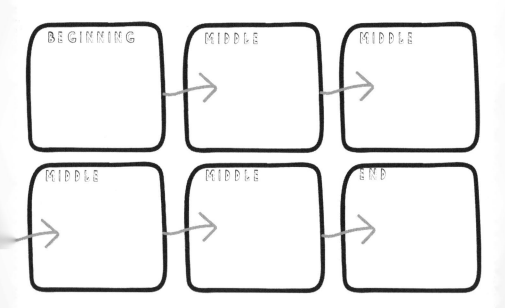

BEGINNING	MIDDLE	MIDDLE
MIDDLE	MIDDLE	END

What will the title be?

_____

WHO WILL VIEW IT?

What will they like about it? Why will they watch it?

_____

_____

_____

SUCCESS?

VIDEO STATS

Date uploaded: _____

Views ____ 👍 ____ 👎 ____

Shares ____   Comments ____   Subscribers ____

How would YOU rate your video out of 10? _____

Would you do anything differently next time?

_____

_____

VIDEO NO. 10

TYPE OF VIDEO:

Vlog / Product Review / Gaming / Funny / Stunts and Skills

What will the topic be?

_____

_____

WHAT'S GOING TO HAPPEN?

How will it start?

What will happen in the middle?

How will it end?

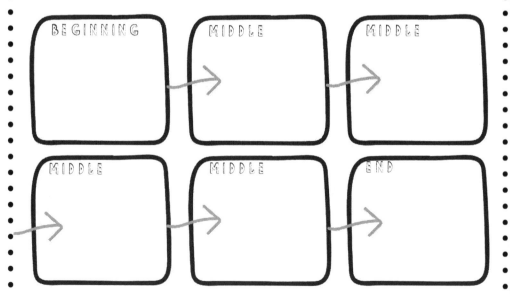

| BEGINNING | MIDDLE | MIDDLE |
| MIDDLE | MIDDLE | END |

What will the title be?

_____

WHO WILL VIEW IT?

What will they like about it? Why will they watch it?

_____

_____

_____

SUCCESS?

VIDEO STATS

Date uploaded: _____

Views _____   👍 _____   👎 _____

Shares _____   Comments _____   Subscribers _____

How would YOU rate your video out of 10? _____

Would you do anything differently next time?

_____

_____

VIDEO NO. 11

TYPE OF VIDEO:

Vlog / Product Review / Gaming / Funny / Stunts and Skills

What will the topic be?

_____

_____

WHAT'S GOING TO HAPPEN?

How will it start?

What will happen in the middle?

How will it end?

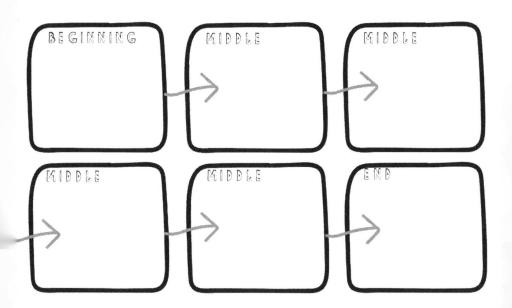

What will the title be?

_____

WHO WILL VIEW IT?

What will they like about it? Why will they watch it?

_____

_____

_____

SUCCESS?

VIDEO STATS

Date uploaded: _____

Views ___ 👍 ___ 👎 ___

Shares ___   Comments ___   Subscribers ___

How would YOU rate your video out of 10? ____

Would you do anything differently next time?

_____

_____

VIDEO NO. 12

TYPE OF VIDEO:

Vlog / Product Review / Gaming / Funny / Stunts and Skills

What will the topic be?

_____

_____

WHAT'S GOING TO HAPPEN?

How will it start?

What will happen in the middle?

How will it end?

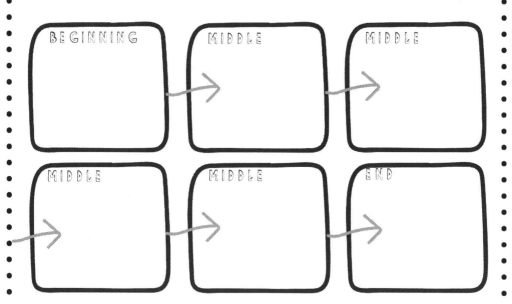

BEGINNING	MIDDLE	MIDDLE

MIDDLE	MIDDLE	END

What will the title be?

_____

WHO WILL VIEW IT?

What will they like about it? Why will they watch it?

_____

_____

_____

SUCCESS?

VIDEO STATS

Date uploaded: _____

Views ____ 👍 ____ 👎 ____

Shares ____ Comments ____ Subscribers ____

How would YOU rate your video out of 10? ____

Would you do anything differently next time?

_____

_____

INDEX

Keep track of all your videos here...

Date	Video Title	Length	Views / Likes / Comments / Shares

Date	Video Title	Length	Views / Likes / Comments / Shares

NOTES